Facilitator's Guide

for use with

Mystie's Activities for Bereaved Children Grades 3 - 5

and

For the Love of Emrys

KIDS' GRIEF RELIEF

Hi, I'm Mystie.
What's
Dragon - You - Down ?

www.KidsGriefRelief.org

A 501(c)(3) NonProfit

Grief Support to Empower Bereaved Children

ISBN: 978-0-9856334-2-4
(softcover book)

Congratulations on deciding to facilitate a student bereavement group!

Your great contribution is giving your students the opportunity to process their grief over the death of a loved one, while empowering them with life affirming skills. This program is not a substitute for professional counseling. It is a program to support students to move through their grief themselves as you create a safe and loving environment.

Validation of their challenging experience, no matter how extreme, is crucial. It creates a foundation of unconditional love and acceptance, which is the perfect environment for the success of this course. The validating conversation helps your students understand that their reactions to the death are normal. It helps them see that no matter how "dire" the situation may look, they have the ability to not only move through their grief, but be stronger for their experience. As you practice empathy instead of sympathy, you place yourself in a position to support your student's journey through grief.

The activities in this program can also create a healing self-dialogue within the child, as well as a healing dialogue between students.

Grief is not an experience students "get over". It's an experience they move through. Ultimately, the death of a loved one becomes integrated into their lives. They can then use this experience to help them gain an awareness of their inner power to move through any of life's challenges.

Our deepest intention is that this course supports each student with the knowledge of the power of Changeless Love within them. Change is inevitable, as realized with the death of a loved one. Yet Love remains forever. It's ongoing expression creates a fulfilling life, moment by moment.

Blessings,
Kids' Grief Relief

Program Guidelines

- This is a grade-specific, *Activity-Based* program which consists of this Facilitator's Guide, and a Student's Booklet of 31 Activities (i.e. ***Mystie's Activities***) which students use to construct their own Activity Book.

- This a a Six-Session Program; ideally one Session per week (we recommend no more than two Sessions per week). The Six Sessions are titled:

  - **What is Grief ?**
  - **Tell Your Story**
  - **My Memories**
  - **I Can Feel Better**
  - **I Choose New Thoughts**
  - **Endings and Celebration**

- The Program is written for groups, and works best when students can interact with each other. It can easily and effectively be used for one child, by selecting activities that do not involve other's participation. We recommend that no more than six students be in a group.

- Each Session contains multiple activities about the specified theme. There are enough activities to last about 45 minutes to one hour per session. The number of activities accomplished is a function of the number of students, the allotted time, the amount of discussion, and the choice to either do the activities verbally or in written form.

- It is recommended that the students receive a folder to store their *Mystie's Activities* book/ pages, and personal photos of their loved one.

- For each Session, the facilitator directs the students to the chosen Activities. Some Activites are only generated by the facilitator, so there is no cooresponding numbered activity in the booklet.

Program Guidelines

- _Mystie's Activities_ are referenced by activity number (e.g. Activity 8). The Activity number is located at the lower corner of each page (e.g. Activity 10A). Remember some student's Activites are only presented in this document (e.g. Activity 1).

- If it's not possible to get all the written activities completed in one session, activities can be done orally, focusing on the goal of the session. For example, in Activity 16 (_Things to Remind Me_), if there isn't enough time for students to write their list, they can orally share their favorite mementos and tell the class where they keep them.

- Collect the folders at the end of each session. The culmination of all the activity sheets becomes each student's personal keepsake awarded at the end of the program. It is a written record of their participation and achievement.

- For each activity, read over the complete procedure before you present it. You know your students best. You may want to skip some steps or add something of your own. Skip any activity that does not fit your student's needs.

- When directed to "read pg.....", either select students to do the reading, or the facilitator can read aloud, as students follow. Note the terms "special person" and "loved one" are used interchangeably in reference to the person for whom the student is grieving.

- Encourage students to bring to class pictures and memorabilia of their loved ones. Always allow time for students to share these items.

- The provided Mystie Mobile is a kinestetic opportunity for students to bend the wings to show how they feel.

- If you have any questions regarding this program, please email us at inquiry@kidsgriefrelief.org

Required Facilitator Materials

(Provided Items in Blue)

For All Six Sessions:

Markers/crayons/pens/pencils

Mystie's Activities for Bereaved Children Grades 3 - 5

Facilitator's Guide

Mystie Mobile

Folder for each student

Additional Needed Materials:

Session#1

Session#2
For the Love of Emrys

Session#3
Game Markers and One Die

Candy for prizes

Session#4
Mystie Mobile

Session#5
Waste Basket

Scrap paper

Hand mirror

Session#6
Battery operated tea-lights for each student

Food & Drinks for students

*Optional: Graduation Gift for each student ***

*Kids' Grief Relief sells special **Mystie** gifts for children who have completed the course.
Go to www.kidsgriefrelief.org/Products.html
to choose and order the most appropriate items for each student.*

CLASS
SYLLABUS

Class Syllabus

Session #1
<u>What Is Grief?</u>

Session #2
<u>Tell Your Story</u>

Session #3
<u>My Memories</u>

Class Syllabus

Session #4
I Can Feel Better

17. Am I Still Dragged-Down?

18. Changeless Love

19. I Know What I Can Do

20. BREATHE

Session #5
I Choose New Thoughts

21. The Power of Thoughts

22. I Am Aware of My Thoughts

23. I Release My Negative Thoughts

24. I Create New Thoughts

25. Frame Yourself !

Session #6
Endings & Celebrations

26. Past, Present & Future

27. I Understand The Grieving Process

28. Letter To My Loved One

29. Letter From My Loved One

30. Ending Celebration

31. Words To Live By

Session 1
<u>What is Grief ?</u>

Objectives

✳ Students gain an understanding of Grief.

✳ Students become comfortable with the natural reactions to a death of someone close to them.

✳ Students recognize their own personal support system.

✳ Students become familiar with other students who are grieving.

Before handing out *Mystie's Activities* :

–Discuss why students are participating in a grief group.
–Discuss the importance of coming to each session.
–Discuss the level of participation: it's their own choice and it's okay not to share.
–Discuss using common courtesies, such as being quiet when someone is speaking, and showing respect to other members.

Session 1
What is Grief ?
Activities 1-8

Mystie's Activities

1A-B. Introduction

2. Getting Aquainted

3A-B. What Is Grief ?

4. Defining My Grief

5. Confidentiality

6. Expressing Grief

7. How My Body Feels

8. My Support People

Activity 1 A-B
Introduction

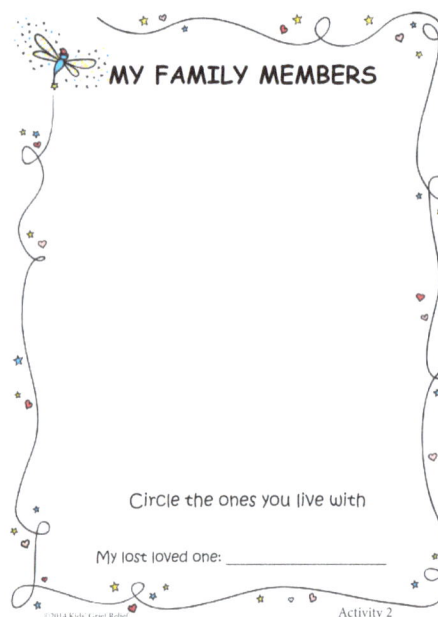

My Special Activity Booklet about _____ and me.

A-1 ©2011 Kids' Grief Relief 5

MY FAMILY MEMBERS

Circle the ones you live with

My lost loved one: _____

©2014 Kids' Grief Relief Activity 2

Procedure:

- Direct children to fill in the blank at the top of the Activity 1A page.

- Direct them to draw a picture of their loved one with themselves.

- Direct students to fill out Activity 1B. Have them include Aunts/Uncles, Grandparents, and Pets.

Activity 2
Getting Aquainted

Hi Kids!
My name is Mystie. I'm a mystical, magical dragonfly from a far away planet.

TIME TO SHARE

What's your name?

What grade are you in?

How old are you?

Who died?

Share your cover picture with your group.

©2013 Kids' Grief Relief

Procedure:

• Read top of page.

• Tell students that whenever they see the heartshaped clock, it's a sign to verbally share with the rest of the group.

• Invite students, one at a time, to answer Mystie's questions, then share their picture with the group.

Activity 3
What Is Grief?

Are you feeling dragged—down because someone you love has died?

I felt dragged—down when my best friend, Darvy, the earth dragonfly, suddenly died. I knew I would never see him again. It felt awful. I couldn't even fly.

Eventually, I felt better.

©2013 Kids' Grief Relief

When I first flew to Earth, I thought Earth dragonflies lived forever like the dragonflies where I come from.

So when I met Darvy, the Earth dragonfly, I thought we would be friends for a long time. But I was wrong. Earth dragonflies have a short life.

Darvy and I had so much fun together! We flew wildly all over the marsh at the edge of the beach, where we lived. We laughed and played all day long. I loved being with him!

Then one day while we were playing dragonfly tag, he died. He suddenly stopped flying and fell to the ground. I was shocked. I felt terrible. I couldn't believe what happened.

We had a funeral, and buried him near a special rock where we used to sit and talk. I cried and cried.

I had a lot of different feelings. Some of the feelings are listed on the next page. What are YOU feeling?

©2014 Kids' Grief Relief   3B

Procedure:

- Read beginning of Activity 3A to introduce the idea of being "*dragged-down*". Invite students to walk around the room looking dragged-down.

- Ask a student to read Activity 3B, which tells about how Mystie, a fictional character, experienced grief.

Activity 4
Defining My Grief

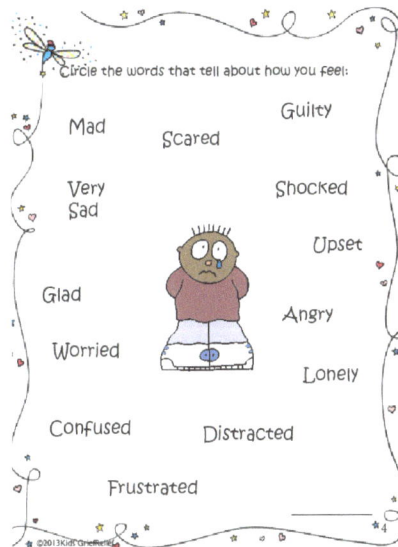

Circle the words that tell about how you feel:

Mad   Scared   Guilty

Very Sad   Shocked

                      Upset

Glad   Angry

Worried   Lonely

Confused   Distracted

Frustrated

©2013 Kids' Grief Relief

Procedure:

- Orally go over each word on this page, making certain students understand the meaning of each listed emotion.

- Direct students to circle each word that describes how they are feeling.

- Students can add other emotions that are not listed.

<u>NOTE</u>
This Activity will be revisited at the beginning of each new session. Different color markers can be used each session to distinguish past from present emotions.

Activity 5
Confidentiality

> Can you share aloud
> why you circled
> those words?
>
> For example,
> "I feel worried because my dad
> is not acting the same."
>
> Everyone grieves differently.
> There's no right or wrong way.
> You are grieving your way. The
> other students in your group are
> grieving the way they need to.
>
> Don't
> talk to students
> outside of your group about
> what's going on within your group.
> Whatever is said, stays in your group.
> It's confidential.
>
> Write your name on the line below, if you
> agree to this. Also write today's date.

©2013 Kids' Grief Relief

Procedure:

- Read top of Activity 5 with students.

- Give students time to share their responses.

- Read middle of page, emphasizing there's no one "right way" to grieve. <u>Tell students the only "wrong" way to greive would be to hurt themselves or others.</u>

- Read words inside the circle. Discuss the importance of keeping confidential what is said in group.

- Students sign and date on the line in the circle.

Activity 6
Expressing Grief

When I was feeling dragged—down about Darvy's death, the beautiful colors in my wings were all muddied up. I had so many feelings.

What colors show your feelings?

For example, what color shows you're sad?   ? Gray?

What color shows you're upset? You're worried?

Would   color in my wings   show how you feel?

©2013 Kids' GriefRelief

Procedure:

- Read Activity 6.

- After students color in Mystie's wings, ask them to tell why they chose their colors.

Activity 7
How My Body Feels

You might also have pains in your body, like a stomach ache or head ache. You might feel extra tired. It's good to talk about how your body is feeling, too.

How does your body feel?

My friend Lark, the dolphin, helped me a lot when I was grieving over Darvy.

©2013 Kids' Grief Relief

Procedure:

- Read top of Activity 7.

- Students discuss how their body feels since the death of their loved one.

- Students can color in the affected areas.

- Ask students if they would like to draw a heart around the affected areas, as a symbol that they know they will eventually feel better.

- Read bottom of Activity 7, which leads to Activity 8 on next page.

Activity 8
My Support People

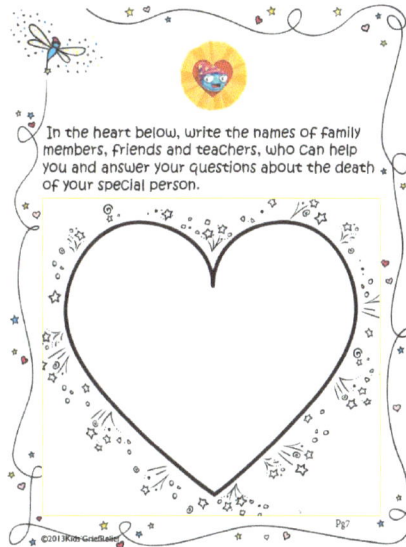

In the heart below, write the names of family members, friends and teachers, who can help you and answer your questions about the death of your special person.

©2013 Kids' GriefRelief   Pg7

Procedure:

- Read top of Activity 8.

- After students have written the names of everyone on their support list, ask them to share their list with the group.

- Ask students to bring to class a photo of their deceased loved one. The picture can be placed on the desk/table, so everyone can see. Allow students the opportunity to talk about the photo.

Session 2
Tell Your Story

Objectives

- Students gain an awareness of another child's grief journey by listening to, or reading aloud, *For the Love of Emrys*.

- Students record and share their own unique story of the death of their loved one.

- Students learn about Compassion and are given the chance to practice it.

Materials Needed:

For the Love of Emrys

Session 2
Tell Your Story

Activities 9-12

Mystie's Activities

9. Reading For the Love of Emrys

10A-D. My Story

11. I Am Compassionate

12. Practicing Compassion

Activity 9
Reading *For the Love of Emrys*

Procedure:

- On top of Activity 9, Mystie asks the students how they are feeling. Allow students time to either write or speak aloud how they are generally doing as they are moving through their grief.

- Revisit Activity 4, using different color markers to distinguish past emotions from present ones.

- Tell Students they will be starting each session this way.

- Take out the book, *For the Love of Emrys.*

Activity 9
Reading *For the Love of Emrys*

continued

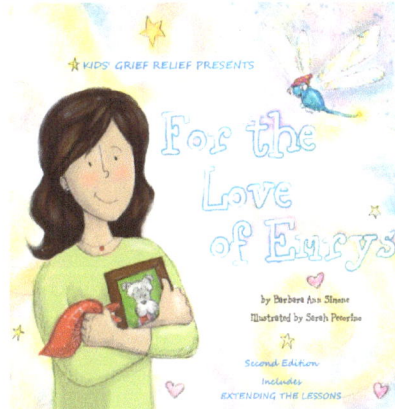

- Show students the bookcover. Point to Mystie, the magical dragonfly, who is with Christina. Ask students who they think has died.(her dog) Ask how Christina will react to the death. (she grieves).

- Tell students that even though the story is sad because of the death of her dog, Emrys, Christina feels better at the end of the story. The author of the story (Barbara Ann Simone) is a real person who lost her dog, Emrys. She wrote this story to share what she discovered about grief.

- Read story. As it is read, ask the students to look for Mystie in the beginning pages of the story, before Emrys dies. (Mystie is in the background of a few pages before she introduces herself to Christina).

- After reading the story ask students what their favorite part was. Next ask what they thought the saddest part was.

Activity 10A-B
My Story

Did you read about my friend Christina? I helped her when her dog died. She was really sad.

At the end of her story, Christina feels a lot better. She knows Emrys will always be in her heart. She has lots of love to share with others; she'll love them for the rest of her life.

10A

Now it's your turn to tell your story about what happened when your loved one died. You can either speak it aloud, or write it down and share what you've written.

TIME TO SHARE

To guide you, Christina tells certain parts of her story, so you can tell the same part OF YOUR story.

Pg9

Procedure:

- Ask a student to pretend he/she is Mystie and read Activity 10A to the other students.

- Ask students if there is any part of the story they would like to dramatize (allow time for this).

- Read Activity 10B to prepare students to tell their story.

Activity 10C-D
My Story

The personal circumstances in each student's experience will determine the amount of detail that can be shared. One sentence, a few sentences, or a drawing might be all a student wants to share for each section. Some sections may be left completely blank. That's fine.

Procedure:

- These two pages of Activity 10C and Activity 10D can be done one section at a time. Ask a student to read the top left side, then the top right side. Give students a chance to write in the box (or not). Continue with each section.

OR

- Read over one page at a time, and allow students to fill in the complete page, then go on to the next full page.

- Ask students to share their story from beginning to end.

Activity 11
I Am Compassionate

Were you a good listener when the other students were telling their story? I hope so!

You had the opportunity to practice COMPASSION.

Compassion comes from your loving heart. It's a warm feeling of understanding that someone is hurting. You take the time to listen to someone tell about their hurt. Listening with a loving heart helps alot.

I showed COMPASSION for
(list the members of your grief group)

Procedure:

- Read Activity 11 with students and direct them to list the names of the other students in the group.

Activity 12
Practicing Compassion

You can also practice Compassion by speaking words which come from your heart. Everyone grieves differently. But having someone care helps a person whose is feeling grief.

Here are some ideas of what to say. Read each one to yourself, then choose one to say to someone else in the group.

"Your _____ loved you a lot. I know you're going to miss her. I bet you have lots of great memories about her.

"I'm sorry to hear about the death of _____. You must miss him very much."

"I know you feel really sad about _____ dying. It's okay to feel sad and upset about it."

"I'm sorry to hear about the death of your _____. I guess this is a hard time for you."

"I feel sad to hear about the death of your _____. I'm here if you need someone to talk to."

Procedure:

- Read Activity 12.

- Direct students to choose one phrase (or create their own) to speak to another student in the group.

Session 3
My Memories

Objectives

✦ Students enjoy sharing special memories of their deceased loved one.

✦ Students reflect about the death of their special loved one.

✦ Students draw a picture of where they believe their loved one has gone.

✦ Students make a list of things they are keeping to remind them of their loved one.

Materials Needed:

Game markers & One Die
Candy for Prizes

Session 3
My Memories

Activities 13-16

Mystie's Activities

13A-B. Roll-A-Memory Game

14. Reflections

15. Where is my Special Loved One now ?

16. Things to Remind Me

Activities 13A-B
Roll-A-Memory Game

Hi Kids! How are you feeling today?

Today I am feeling _____

On the next page there's a game to play.
You each have your own board.
Directions:
1. Choose a marker.
2. Decide the order of players.
3. First person rolls the dice and moves that many spaces along their board.
4. Read the question on the square. If you can answer it, speak it aloud. Circle the number on the square.
5. If it's a question you can't answer, put an X on the square and skip over it the next time around.
6. Play a few rounds till you have at least 8 numbers circled.

7. Remember to practice Compassion when you play this game!

©2013 Kids' Grief Relief   Pg.14

1	2	3	4	5
What is the first and last name of your special person?	Did your special person teach you anything?	Do you know your special person's birthday? (month/day/year)	Was your special person buried or cremated?	Did your special person like to wear jewelry? What kind?
6	7	8	9	10
Describe a special holiday spent with your special person.	Tell about the last time you saw your special person.	GET A PRIZE!	Tell about a funny moment with your special person.	Describe a trip you took with your special person.
11	12	13	14	15
Tell about what kind of clothes your special person liked to wear.	GIVE A PRIZE TO SOMEONE IN THE ROOM!	What kind of music did your special person enjoy?	What kind of movies did your special person like to watch?	Did your special person ever have a pet?
16	17	18	19	20
Did your special person have a favorite saying - what is it?	Tell about a sad memory with your favorite person.	Tell about some of the people who loved your special person.	What one thing always makes you think about your special person?	What's your favorite photo of your special person? Describe it.
21	22	23	24	25
GET A PRIZE!	What time of day do you feel "dragged-down" over the death of your special person?	What's the one thing you will miss MOST about your special person?	Do you feel peaceful about the way your special person was buried? Why?	Tell about a gift you gave your special person.

Pg.15

Procedure:

- On top of Activity 13A, Mystie asks the students how they are feeling. Allow students time to either write or speak aloud how they are generally doing as they are moving through their grief. Revisit Activity 4 using different color markers.

- Read directions for game on the second half of Activity 13A.

- Students play game, which is Activity 13B.

- Reward each child for completing the game with a candy prize.

30

Activity 14
Reflections

My favorite memory of my friend Darvy the earth dragonfly, is playing tag with him.
He was very fast, but I usually outflew him!
We laughed and laughed as we played together.
I think a lot about Darvy.

I wonder what other adventures we could have had together.

I try to remember that he is happy in dragonfly heaven.

I understand why he died, though I don't like it.

I want to always remember how he made me laugh.

I learned a lot about myself after he died.

I am a mystical, magical dragonfly who misses my best friend so much!

I wonder _____.

I try _____.

I understand _____.

I want _____.

I learned _____.

I am _____.

Procedure:

- Refer back to Activity 3B, where Mystie shared how she experienced grief.

- Ask a student to read the top of Activity 14.

- Under the picture, go over each statement with different students reading each statement.

- Direct students to share their thoughts for each statement on the bottom of Activity 14. Students can either write or verbally speak their ideas.

Activity 15
Where is my
Special Loved One now?

I believe Darvy's spirit is somewhere in dragonfly heaven.
Christina believes Emrys' spirit is in heaven, too.

Where do you believe your special person's spirit is?
Draw a picture of what you think it looks like.

©2013 Kids' Grief Relief

Procedure:

- Start a discussion about where the students now believe their special person's spirit is.

- Read Activity 15.

- Ask students to draw a picture to demonstrate their belief.

Activity 16
Things To Remind Me

Here's a picture of Christina holding a picture of her pet dog Emrys, who died. She's also holding his bandanna, which she saved to remind her of him.

What special things do you have to remind yourself about your special someone who died? Make a list.

1 ⭐   2 ⭐

3 ⭐   4 ⭐

5 ⭐   6 ⭐

Procedure:

- Read Activity 16.

- Direct students to write their list on the paper.

- If there is time, ask students to share their lists.

Session 4
I Can Feel Better

Objectives

- Students manipulate a Mystie mobile to demonstrate how they are moving through grief.

- Students become aware of their ability to continue to love their special loved one.

- Students choose wise ways to handle their different emotions, and share their ideas with the group.

- Students learn the value of breathing as a tool to help them with their grief.

Materials Needed:
Mystie Mobile

Session 4
I Can Feel Better

Activities 17-20

Mystie's Activities

17. Am I Still Dragged-Down ?

18. Changeless Love

19A-B. I Know What I Can Do

20. BREATHE

Activity 17
Am I Still Dragged-Down?

Hi Kids! How are you feeling today?

Today I am feeling _____

Look at the mobile of me. Can you bend my wings to show everyone how you've been feeling the past week?

TIME TO SHARE

When you're grieving over someone, parts of you may be happy, yet parts may be still sad or upset.

Use my four wings to show your feelings.

©2013 Kids' Grief Relief   Pg.19

Procedure:

- On top of Activity 17, Mystie again asks the students how they are feeling. Allow students time to either write or speak aloud how they are generally doing as they move through their grief. Revisit Activity 4 using different color markers.

- Read over the rest of the page and give out a Mystie mobile to one of the students. Allow student the time needed to express him/herself with Mystie's four wings. Repeat for all students.

- When each student has had the opportunity to use the mobile, you can continue to the next activity.

Activity 18
Changeless Love

Through her grief, Christina learned that the love in her heart is changeless. She will always love Emrys. She loved him when he was alive, and continues to love him even though he is gone.

Your love for your special person will be inside your heart forever, too.

Look at the heart below.

On the left side of the heart, write about how you showed love for your special person before he/she died.

On the right side write or draw pictures of how you show you still love him/her.

©2013 Kids' Grief Relief   Pg. 28

Procedure:

- Read over Activity 18 with students. Start a discussion concerning how each student demonstrated *Love* for their special loved one when he/she was alive.

- Brainstorm with students to think about new rituals they can create to honor their loved one (planting flowers, writing a song, creating murals, etc...)

- Direct students to fill out both sides of the heart.

Activity 19A-B
I Know What I Can Do

Loving yourself by doing things you enjoy can help you move through grief. Think about ways you can help yourself to feel better. You can draw pictures or write down your ideas.

When I feel sad I can	When I feel worried I can
When I feel scared I can	When I feel angry I can
When I feel upset I can	When I feel _____ I can

©2013 Kids' Grief Relief   Pg. 21

What's your favorite thing to do? Close your eyes for a moment, and pretend you are doing it.

Now, color and decorate my wings to show how you feel when you're doing your favorite thing.

I know you can't fly like me, but you can feel like you're flying, when you're doing something you really enjoy.

©2013 Kids' Grief Relief   Pg. 22

Procedure:

- Read over Activity 19A with students. Brainstorm ways students can express their dragged-down feelings in positive ways. Students can write down their ideas as they agree with what is stated. For example, if one student talks about "playing music" when he feels mad, any other student can write down "playing music" in their box. Encourage students to help each other come up with some ideas!

- Read over Activity 19B, and give students time to color in Mystie's wings to demonstrate how they feel.

Activity 20
BREATHE

Here's another way to help yourself when you're feeling dragged—down.

It's all about BREATHING.

When you take the time to control how you breathe, you can help yourself handle some of the dragged—down emotions of grief. You will feel more relaxed and calm. Your body gets the air it needs to calm yourself down. That feels good.

Pg.23

©2013 Kids' GriefRelief

Procedure:

- Read over Activity 20 to introduce the idea of using breath to help ourselves when we are feeling dragged-down.

- Ask students to relax and listen to you as you read the script on the next two pages.

Begin...

Let's relax right now. First, let your body relax a bit. Reach up, high above your head, stretching your arms... stretching your body very tall. Now let your arms relax. relax. Place them at your sides, loosely.

Do the same thing again, but this time, breathe in as you reach up. Stretch.... and now breathe out as you relax and place your arms at your sides.
One more stretch, arms up, breathing in... and relax, arms down, breathing out.
Just sit now, letting your arms rest at your sides.
See how your breathing can relax you by taking slow, deep breaths. Breathe in.... hold your breath.... and now breathe out, slowly. Breathe in.... and out.
Keep breathing deeply and slowly.

Continue the breathing relaxation for children.

Place one hand on your chest and one hand on your stomach. Feel both of your hands moving up and out as you breathe in... and down as you breathe out. Feel your hands moving with your chest and stomach, gently moving in and out with each breath.
(pause)

Another way your breathing can relax you is to breathe like different animals. Do you know how a dog pants? Breathe in.... and now as you breathe out, pant, ha ha ha ha ha ha ha.Breathe in.... pant, ha ha ha ha ha. Breathe in... pant.
Imagine that you are like a cat purring. Breathe in... and as you breathe out, purr. Breathe in.... purr. Breathe in... purr.
Now as you breathe, you can sigh, and relax. Breathe in.... and sigh as you breathe out. Breathe in.... sigh. Breathe in.... sigh.
Just relax now for a moment, feeling your body relax. Your arms and legs are very loose and relaxed.

Continue the breathing relaxation for children.

Now you can imagine that your body is like a balloon filling up as you breathe in, and emptying as you breathe out. Let your ribs expand out to the sides, like a balloon, expanding... and then let the air out, like a balloon that is emptying. The balloon expands.... and then the air goes out.

You can even imagine that you are blowing up a balloon. Imagine that you breathe air into your lungs, and then when you breathe out through your mouth, imagine that you are blowing up a balloon. Each breath you blow out makes the balloon get even bigger. Imagine filing the balloon as it gets bigger and bigger with each breath out. Breathe in... and then blow up the balloon even more. Bigger... bigger.... bigger.

Imagine letting go of the balloon, so it flies around the room as the air escapes. Feel your body relaxing just like a limp, empty balloon. Continue the breathing relaxation for children.

And now, see how slowly you can breathe out. First breathe in.... and now breathe out very slowly... out... out.... out. When you can't breathe out any more air, breathe in again, and then very slowly breathe out. For the next few moments, just relax, resting. It feels good to relax. Enjoy this calm feeling.
(pause)

Now you are finished this breathing relaxation for children. Stretch your muscles if you want to, and let your body wake up. When you are totally awake, you can get back to the rest of your day.

http://www.innerhealthstudio.com/
breathing-relaxation-for-children.html

Session 5
I Choose New Thoughts

Objectives

- Students become aware that their thoughts have a direct effect on their experience.

- Students uncover their own negative thoughts in order to release them.

- Students create new, empowering thoughts about themselves.

- Students create new, powerful affirmations.

- Students gain a greater sense of their inner strengths to move through grief.

Materials Needed:

Waste Basket
Scrap Paper
Hand Mirror

Session 5
I Choose New Thoughts

Activities 21-25

Mystie's Activities

21A-B. The Power of Thought

22. I Am Aware of My Thoughts

23. I Release My Negative Thoughts

24. I Create New Thoughts

25. Frame Yourself!

Activity 21A-B
The Power of Thought

Hi Kids! How are you feeling today?

Today I am feeling _____

When I was grieving over the death of Darvy the earth dragonfly, Lark reminded me that my thoughts had a lot to do with how I was feeling. The more positive my thoughts were, the better I felt.

Here's what Lark shared with me. I am excited to share it with you.

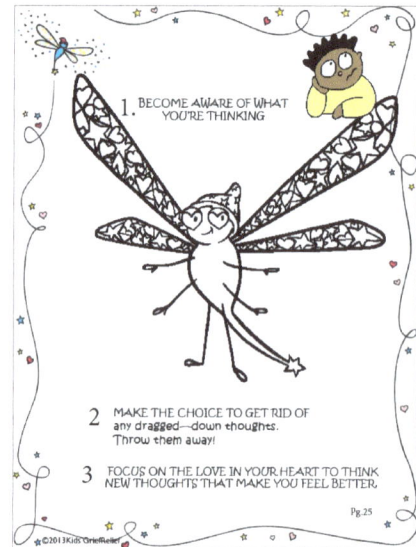

1. BECOME AWARE OF WHAT YOU'RE THINKING

2. MAKE THE CHOICE TO GET RID OF any dragged—down thoughts. Throw them away!

3. FOCUS ON THE LOVE IN YOUR HEART TO THINK NEW THOUGHTS THAT MAKE YOU FEEL BETTER.

Procedure:

- On top of Activity 21A, Mystie again asks the students how they're feeling. Allow students time to either write or speak aloud how they are generally doing as they move through their grief. Revisit Activity 4 using different color markers.

- Read #1 on Activity 21B. Direct students to underline the word "**aware**", and discuss its definition.

- Read #2 and direct students to underline the word "**choice**", and discuss its definition.

- Read #3 and direct students to underline the word "**focus**", and discuss its definition.

Activity 22
I Am Aware of My Thoughts

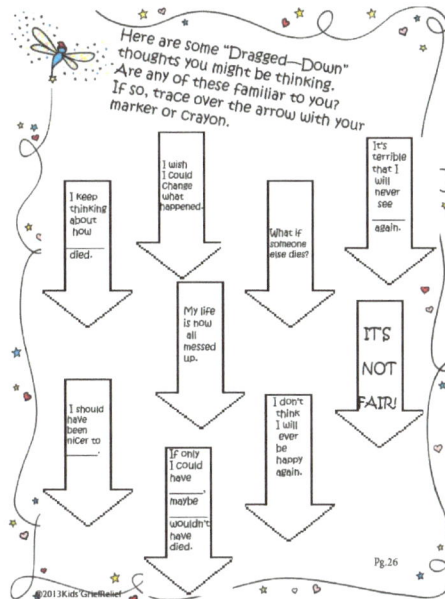

Here are some "Dragged—Down" thoughts you might be thinking. Are any of these familiar to you? If so, trace over the arrow with your marker or crayon.

I keep thinking about how ___ died.

I wish I could change what happened.

What if someone else dies?

It's terrible that I will never see ___ again.

My life is now all messed up.

IT'S NOT FAIR!

I should have been nicer to ___

If only I could have ___ maybe ___ wouldn't have died.

I don't think I will ever be happy again.

Pg.26

©2013 Kids' Grief Relief

Procedure:

- Tell students they are now going to practice #1 from the previous Activity: **Becoming aware of what they are thinking.**

- Read over top of Activity 22.

- Ask different students to read the words in each arrow.

- Students outline the arrows which describe their thoughts.

- Older students may come up with different thoughts and should be directed to write them down on this page.

Activity 23
I Release My Negative Thoughts

Which Dragged—Down thoughts
are you ready to get rid of?
Write them on the arrows below.
Then count to three, take a deep breath,
and THROW THEM AWAY!

And keep them in the trash! Pg. 27

©2013 Kids' Grief Relief

Procedure:

- Tell students since they are now aware of their negative, Trash Thoughts, they can choose to release them, and not think them anymore.

- Read over top of Activity 23. This activity can be done in several ways:

   A. Students write down three Trash Thoughts.
   B. Students write down their trash thoughts on separate pieces of paper, then throw them away in a real trash can.
   C. Students do A&B.
   D. Sharing their Trash Thoughts with the group is optional.

46

Activity 24
I Create New Thoughts

Here are some of my Dragon—Fly thoughts you can think as you focus on the love in your heart.

Can you say these aloud?

1. I am brave.

2. I am smart enough to understand what happened.

3. It feels good to talk to others about what happened.

4. I have my own unique feelings about death.

5. I have special memories of _____ that I will always treasure.

6. I like who I am.

7. I am grateful for all the people who love me.

8. I am a powerful kid!

Pg. 28

©2013 Kids' GriefRelief

Procedure:

- Tell students they are now ready for step #3 from Activity 24 -

  FOCUS ON THE LOVE IN YOUR HEART TO THINK NEW THOUGHTS THAT MAKE YOU FEEL BETTER

- Invite different students to read the positive affirmations.

- Go around the group and ask each student to come up with other positive statements about themselves and their lives.

Activity 25
Frame Yourself !

Write a Dragon—Fly thought for each of
the four sides of the frame below.
Draw a picture of yourself in the frame.

©2013 Kids' Grief Relief   30

Procedure:

• Read top of Activity 25. Direct students to think of four positive statements about themselves. Encourage students to start each statement with "I Am".

• Students write down their positive statements and draw a picture of themselves in the frame.

• Using a hand-mirror, invite each student to look in the mirror, then speak aloud the four affirmations listed on their frame.

NOTE
Tell students they have one session left, and remind them to bring in a picture of their deceased loved one for the ending celebration.

48

"...A 'healing space' is where the bereaved child is given the opportunity to speak to others without any judgement, receiving validation for his or her many feelings and thoughts associtiated with grief. As a dialogue opens up, the child begins the process of leading *themself* through healing"...

"...Eventually, the grieving child is open to receive an understanding that all the thoughts and feelings of grief are a "normal" part of life. The child gives audience for a compassionate adult to support and lead him or her in finding their inner strength to heal. Understanding this lead role is a critical ingredient of the spiritual and emotional growth of the child"...

from *The Evolution of Child Bereavement*
by Kids' Grief Relief

Session 6
Endings and Celebration

Objectives

✦ Students share what they have learned about grief.

✦ Students create a ceremony to honor their loved one.

✦ Students experience some closure in their relationship with their loved one.

✦ Students share in a celebration as an ending of their experience in the group.

Materials Needed:

Battery operated tea-lights for each student
Scissors
Food and Drink for each student
Optional Graduation Gift for each student

(e.g. available from Kids' Grief Relief - see pg.4)

Session 6
Endings and Celebration

Activities 26-30

Mystie's Activities

26. Past, Present, and Future

27. I Understand the Grieving Process

28. Letter To My Loved One

29. Letter From My Loved One

30. Ending Celebration

Activity 26
Past, Present and Future

Hi Kids! How are you feeling today?

Today I am feeling _____

Things have changed in your life.
Can you share some things that are
different since the death of your loved one?

Can you share some things that have
stayed the same?

What are some things you're looking
forward to this coming year?

TIME TO SHARE

Pg. 30

©2013 Kids GriefRelief

Procedure:

- On top of Activity 26, Mystie again asks the students how they are feeling. Allow students time to either write or speak aloud how they are generally doing as they are moving through their grief. Revisit Activity 4 using different color markers.

- Read the second part of Activity 26, one section at a time.

- Give students time to orally answer each section.

- Remind students to practice Compassion by listening with their heart as each student speaks, and speaking kind words to each other during this activity and hopefully afterwards, as well.

Activity 27
I Understand the Grieving Process

You've done a great job learning how to deal with the death of your special person!

Here are some statements about grief.
If you agree with the statement, draw one heart next to it.
If you really, really agree with it, draw two hearts next to it.

1. It's okay to cry when you feel sad.

2. It's normal to be upset and worried when someone you love has died.

3. Everyone grieves the same way.

4. I know it's okay to tell someone that I don't feel well because I am grieving.

5. I will miss _____ for a long time.

6. I can be happy again, even though _____ had died.

7. Hiding my feelings is a good way to feel better.

8. My positive thoughts help me feel better.

9. Acting out in school or at home is a good way to express grief.

10. Taking time to breath and relax helps me when I feel upset.

Pg. 31

©2013 Kids' Grief Relief

Procedure:

- Read top of Activity 27 together.

- Students can do this page by themselves,
          OR
- Go over each statement, one at a time. Discuss the statement and allow the students to answer each one honestly.

Note
This page helps the facilitator assess how each student has understood the grieving process.

Activity 28
Letter To My Loved One

> Dear_____
>
> _____
> _____
> _____
> _____
> _____
> _____
> _____
> _____
> _____
> _____
>
> Love Always,
> _____
>
> Pg. 32

Procedure:

- Direct students to write a letter to their deceased special person. Tell students they can <u>choose</u> to share the letter at the ending celebration during this final session.

Note
Discuss the idea of putting their letter to their loved one in a special place. They may want to keep it in a decorated container or frame it for their room or home. Perhaps they want to bury it.

Activity 29
Letter <u>From</u> My Loved One

Procedure:

- Ask students to pretend to be their special person and write a letter from their special person to themselves. Again, they can <u>choose</u> to share the letter during the ending celebration.

Note

Some students may need some writing prompts.

Here are some suggestions:

"I always wanted to tell you..."

"I wish you could have..."

"What I really miss is...

"I'm feeling...."

"When I think about you I..."

Activity 30
Ending Celebration

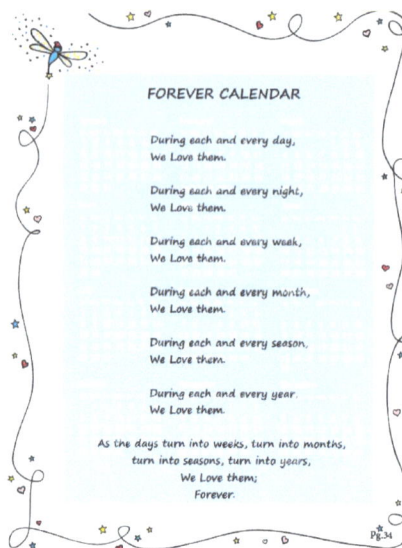

FOREVER CALENDAR

During each and every day,
We Love them.

During each and every night,
We Love them.

During each and every week,
We Love them.

During each and every month,
We Love them.

During each and every season,
We Love them.

During each and every year,
We Love them.

As the days turn into weeks, turn into months,
turn into seasons, turn into years,
We Love them;
Forever.

Pg.34

Procedure:

- Give each student a battery operated candle (provided).

- Direct them to write the name of their loved one on the plastic side (sharpies work best).

- Create an empty space on a table, where the students can place their candles in a circle. Students can place photos of their loved one next to their candle.

- One at a time, ask the students to turn their candle on.

- Remind them that the light of the candle represents the love and light in their hearts, which will be present for their loved for the rest of their lives.

- As the students light their candles, they may read one of both letters.

continued...

Activity 30
Ending Celebration
(Continued)

- When all candles are lit, and each student has had the opportunity to read their letters, read aloud together the *Forever Calendar* on Activity 30.

- After the poem is read, ask students to turn their candle off, allowing them to keep the candle as a special rememberance of their loved one.

- Tell students that in honor of their loved ones, and in honoring their committment to move through grief, there will be a celebration with food and drink.

- Hand out "Graduation Gift" (optional).

- ENJOY!

Note
Kids' Grief Relief offers special mementos for students who have completed this course (e.g. Mystie Bracelet or Keychain).

Activity 31A-B
Words To Live By

Bye Kids! I'm leaving you these powerful Heart-Words to say anytime you're feeling some grief.

Say thes words over and over until you begin to feel the POWER inside you. Then go ahead and have a good day!

The Power of my heart is strong
It gently guides me all day long.
If I feel sad throughout the day
This Love reminds me, I'm still okay!

Even though my life has changed
Since _____ has gone away,
There is one thing that's always there
It's Love inside my heart to share.

I AM A POWERFUL KID!

Procedure:

- As students end their celebration, invite them to read the top half of Activity 31A.

- One at a time, ask students to read the words inside the frame.

- Direct students to write their name in the star on Activity 31B.

- As each student says, "I am a powerful kid!", all the other students reply, "You *are* a powerful kid!"

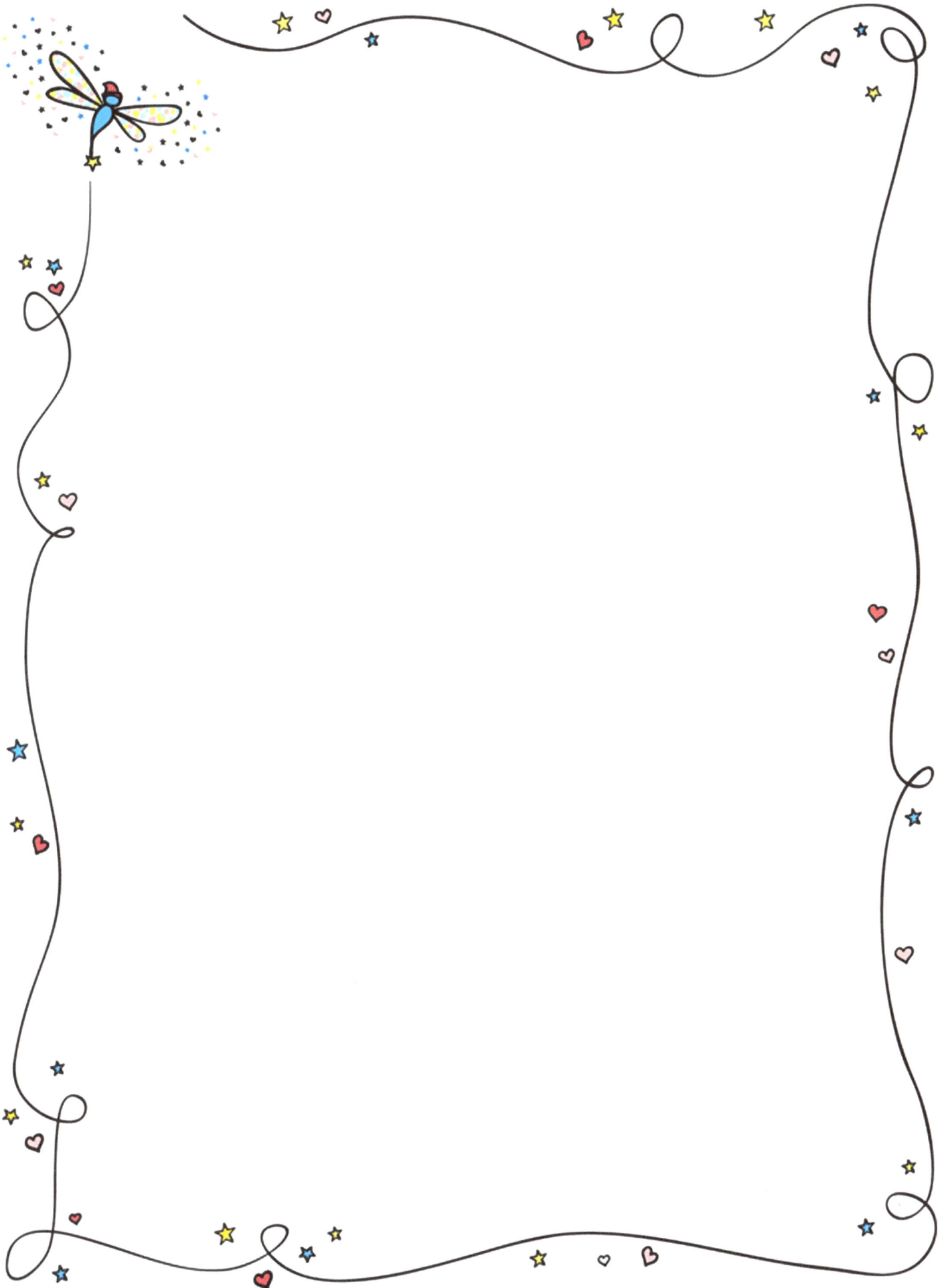

APPENDIX I
SPECIAL ACTIVITIES

(Downloadable from www.KidsGriefRelief.Org)

The following Activities can be used during any of the six sessions.

Some are specific to a time of year, others are special topics discussed in more depth than the session's activities.

They are all available for free !

Simply go to
www. KidsGriefRelief.org
and click on
"Downloads"

APPENDIX I
SPECIAL ACTIVITIES

Mystie tells tips on how
to feel like you're flying

Mystie's Magical
Message to Children

Remembering Someone
Special

Another Magical
Message from Mystie

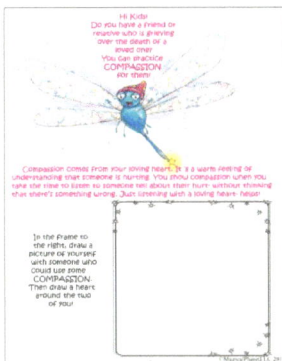

Mystie teaches
Practicing Compassion

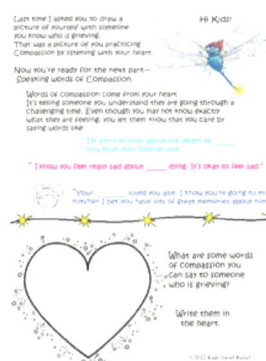

Mystie's Words of
Compassion

Mystie and Memory

Mystie's "I AM" Mirror

Mystie's Valentines Day Message

Mystie talks about Cremation

It's OK to have a "Dragged-Down" Day

Mystie asks, "What are you Thinking?"

APPENDIX I
SPECIAL ACTIVITIES (continued)

Mystie says remember
to honor yourself

Mystie talsk about
Gratitude and Grief

Mystie talks about
back to school time

Mystie explains that
Sharing is Caring

Mystie talks about
Self-Worth

Mystie talks about
Giving Thanks

Mystie's Holiday Special

Mystie talks about starting a new year

Mystie talks about putting your I AM first

Mystie talks about the Greatest Strength of All

Mystie shows Parents some Healing Themes

Mystie asks "What's Changed?"

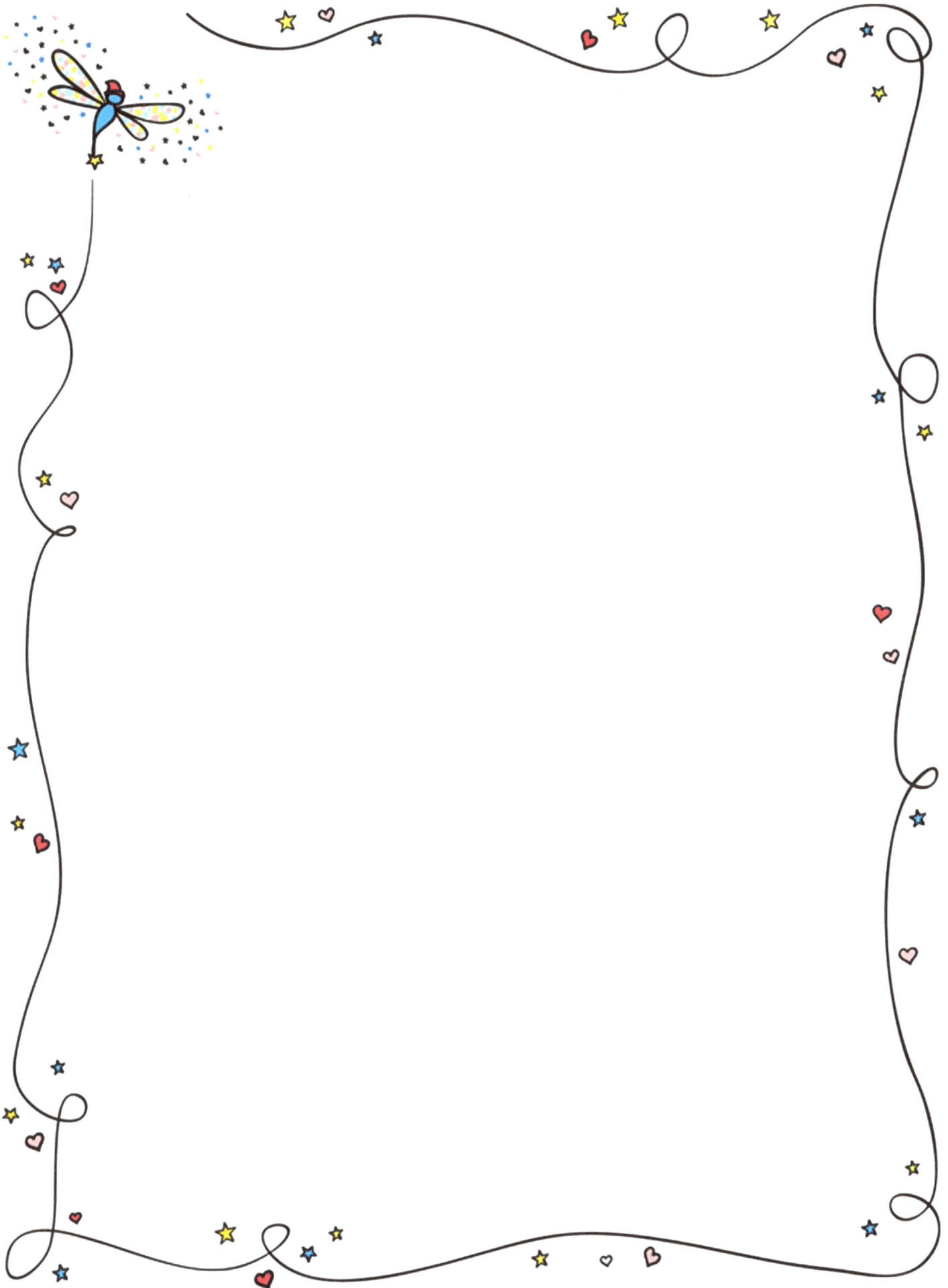

NOTES

www.ingramcontent.com/pod-product-compliance
Lightning Source LLC
LaVergne TN
LVHW072106070426
835509LV00002B/38